RAGS OF NIGHT IN OUR MOUTHS

THE HUGH MacLENNAN POETRY SERIES

Editors: Allan Hepburn and Carolyn Smart

Waterglass Jeffery Donaldson

All the God-Sized Fruit Shawna Lemay

Chess Pieces David Solway

Giving My Body to Science Rachel Rose

The Asparagus Feast S.P. Zitner

The Thin Smoke of the Heart Tim Bowling

What Really Matters Thomas O'Grady

A Dream of Sulphur Aurian Haller

Credo Carmine Starnino

Her Festival Clothes Mavis Jones

The Afterlife of Trees Brian Bartlett

Before We Had Words S.P. Zitner

Bamboo Church Ricardo Sternberg

Franklin's Passage David Solway

The Ishtar Gate Diana Brebner

Hurt Thyself Andrew Steinmetz

The Silver Palace Restaurant Mark Abley

Wet Apples, White Blood Naomi Guttman

Palilalia Jeffery Donaldson

Mosaic Orpheus Peter Dale Scott

Cast from Bells Suzanne Hancock

Blindfold John Mikhail Asfour

Particles Michael Penny

A Lovely Gutting Robin Durnford

The Little Yellow House Heather Simeney MacLeod

Wavelengths of Your Song Eleonore Schönmaier

But for Now Gordon Johnston

Some Dance Ricardo Sternberg

Outside, Inside Michael Penny

The Winter Count Dilys Leman
Tablature Bruce Whiteman
Trio Sarah Tolmie
hook nancy viva davis halifax
Where We Live John Reibetanz
The Unlit Path Behind the House Margo Wheaton
Small Fires Kelly Norah Drukker
Knots Edward Carson
The Rules of the Kingdom Julie Paul
Dust Blown Side of the Journey Eleonore Schönmaier
slow war Benjamin Hertwig
The Art of Dying Sarah Tolmie
Short Histories of Light Aidan Chafe
On High Neil Surkan
Translating Air Kath MacLean
The Night Chorus Harold Hoefle
Look Here Look Away Look Again Edward Carson
Delivering the News Thomas O'Grady
Grotesque Tenderness Daniel Cowper
Rail Miranda Pearson
Ganymede's Dog John Emil Vincent
The Danger Model Madelaine Caritas Longman
A Different Wolf Deborah-Anne Tunney
rushes from the river disappointment stephanie roberts
A House in Memory David Helwig
Side Effects May Include Strangers Dominik Parisien
Check Sarah Tolmie
The Milk of Amnesia Danielle Janess
Field Guide to the Lost Flower of Crete Eleonore
    Schönmaier
Unbound Gabrielle McIntire
Ripping down half the trees Evan J
whereabouts Edward Carson

Rags of Night
in Our Mouths

MARGO WHEATON

McGill-Queen's University Press
Montreal & Kingston • London • Chicago

© Margo Wheaton 2022

ISBN 978-0-2280-1116-3 (paper)
ISBN 978-0-2280-1358-7 (ePDF)
ISBN 978-0-2280-1359-4 (ePUB)

Legal deposit second quarter 2022
Bibliothèque nationale du Québec

Printed in Canada on acid-free paper that is 100% ancient forest free
(100% post-consumer recycled), processed chlorine free

Funded by the Government of Canada | Financé par le gouvernement du Canada

Canada Council for the Arts | Conseil des arts du Canada

We acknowledge the support of the Canada Council for the Arts.

Nous remercions le Conseil des arts du Canada de son soutien.

Library and Archives Canada Cataloguing in Publication

Title: Rags of night in our mouths / Margo Wheaton.

Names: Wheaton, Margo, author.

Series: Hugh MacLennan poetry series.

Description: Series statement: The Hugh MacLennan poetry series |
Poems.

Identifiers: Canadiana (print) 2021039384X | Canadiana (ebook)
20210393904 | ISBN 9780228011163 (softcover) |
ISBN 9780228013587 (PDF) | ISBN 9780228013594 (ePUB)

Classification: LCC PS8595.H3675 R34 2022 | DDC C811/.6—dc23

This book was typeset by Marquis Interscript in 9.5/13 Sabon.

CONTENTS

I

Perhaps knowledge, family, stays harboured in our bodies.
Basma Kavanagh

I want not to have lost what I am looking for now.
F. Alex Pierce

RAGS OF NIGHT IN OUR MOUTHS

(For my father)

I

We've assembled again at the kitchen table, heads
bobbing. Deep in ancient rivers of chat.

Tasselled lavender bunches and chamomile
hung from ceiling rafters: earth candles for our table.

Bricks of wrapped amber papers seasons-
old on the old pine chair.

Out back, the reedy dark runs all the way
to the property line.

Five black pines you planted
are defiant flags.

Silence in the belly of the breathing house. Night so deep,
it's reaching through rooms as if searching its pockets.

II

The good, leafy dark inside the kitchen: turn the lights off.
Hear everything breathing this way.

In the morning, porch so cold, it's creaking. Railings
dressed in ice-stiff shawls of frost.

Two a.m. My stepmother's in the kitchen crying.
Vodka in half-filled glasses the colour of tears.

This plastic lamp attached to the wall above your shoulder
is carving a path through the darkness too narrow to walk.

Wanted to give you something of some of the stories here:
can't think of the details;

only the rhythms,
the songs.

III

We say love, affection, security. Warmth. Then
choke, rags of night in our mouths.

I want the unstirred bowl of dark at the base of the poplar
past the shed. The wordlessness of its leaves turning over.

In the morning, my sister and I will drive the big marsh
that's taken the lives of some in the family.

Walk grassy seams
where they balanced there.

The jewellery box and hand-held mirrors
that once adorned the dresser

shattered
by the bottle's curve.

Years after everything's walked away,
I'm still here. Trying to jimmy the locked barn door.

IV

Generations of black moods fill the kitchen
like smoke – let's escape by surrender:

make a white flag from the cloth
of everything that's been lost.

Weeds you call them.
Garbage trees.

In the lawless arms of box elders at the side of the house,
winged seed-pods dangle like earrings.

Tawny pelt of an old mink coat
hanging from a closet door;

it's breathing,
reeking of better days.

The restless gnaw of wanting to walk
the field of family history;

throw heels of bread to the ghosts
that wait.

This half-shadow of bannister rungs on the wall beside
the staircase is a ladder to someplace without ground or sky.

V

Bald, unblinking winter. The worst in years.
Cold winds pressing walls like age.

Wood stove's the heart of the house. Rooms
sticky with sweat and fear.

The chainmail lattice of ice-stilled dogwood thickets
shielding the porch: silvered by a streetlight's stare.

Floating from a horserace pass in a wallet, the blue
signature of a grandfather wary of walls –

the distance unstalled
hearts can run.

This sudden kick of pain's a pull
on reins no-one told me I held.

These tongues reached for fire and water. Amber cradles
where some drowned, rocking their lives.

VI

Sleepless, she paces the kitchen: appliances
singing, still speaking the past.

Don't run from this slow-burning building. Memory's
black billows scalding your lungs.

Inside a drawer lined with debris, rosehips rolling.
Lemon balm. Tinctures made to calm and soothe.

How you carefully hook through a story the same way
your feet could find paths across wet river stones.

Lord help me Jesus on the radio. That lonely
cigarette voice in our ears. Smell of time on our skin.

But heartbreak's the sound that cracks
it all open, can unjam

every window,
each door.

VII

Like blood, the warmth in a red and black checkered jacket
felled like a carcass at the foot of the stairs.

Dark pine baseboards tram the length of floors,
protecting walls. When did life become unkind?

From up here, sky's so pure: a skim-blue fleck of eggshell.
Mind the knife-edge of your thoughts.

In a bedroom window, a gothic nest
of rain-lashed elder branches. Night's tantrum.

I've come for the light. Pooling, now, like water
spilled across the floor. May it

fill each emptying room
with brimming.

VIII

The scuffed green tile in the bathroom knows. Carries
the bowl of our scent in its hands.

What does staring at anything serve? Nothing
here but outmoded worlds:

time-browned snow globes spinning
in air.

Quiet. Let's rest before this caramel fire of knotted floors.
My heart's asleep in rings and whorls.

Wrestling an upstairs window, my fingers come back
wearing decades: charcoal-greyed;

I'm learning to carry
the look of them stained.

Years of your elbows' nightly pilgrimage across the table's
finally skinned the finish off.

There's an honesty
in naked wood.

IX

At noon, varnished light the hue of rotting peaches
combs through the snow-filled maple;

rests like a spoon on the side
of the shed.

Your abrupt blue-mirrored gaze starts
swimming up in every room. Cast inside the air like lures.

Wrap me in the undersides of birch leaves keeled
by waves of wind;

like silver boats, lives
upturn.

Say it now. Your actions speak it, clear
as the minute after gunshot:

the unsaid, one
resounding word.

It's safe to sleep. Cover your eyes with thoughts
of your last abandoned flannel shirt,

the way field dirt
was silk in your hands.

X

My grandmother's bones hover
above this bed, obtrusive as guardian angels:

open eyes. Frozen
moons.

The warm, needled press of Christmas night.
We're sitting stiffly,

wreathed together. Regarding each
other like neighbouring towns.

Out back, a ring of snow-lined conifers are sentries
guarding the laughter we buried like coins in the garden.

Loneliness has been here
so long, it's a tenant.

I hear it at night,
crying all through the yard.

A white arm withdrawing itself
from a maw of dark above the piano.

I remember a Disney dog figurine.
Its plastic back. Nicotine.

In photos, bones carry her. That grimace,
that set in the jaw.

Fingers that lifted bottles, flew upset, harried
as crows in wind: the same ones pressed and stilled the keys.

Above our heads, the minute hand moves:
an anonymous skater gliding on a pond beyond us.

It's afternoon. Let's sit for a while; clock-wound,
the world will abbreviate tongues,

watch the sun lengthen
walls.

XII

Clumps of red, shrivelled berries freighting
branch-tips of the rowan tree.

Abundance
is a mountain of hands.

One grandmother
one grandfather:

this tickle of sibilant breath in my mouth when
I say their names: that's all I know.

In conversations, they flowed like ghosts, like
water, like smell.

Respectability's a painted
bucket. Heavy with holes.

Her windows were sheathed in Victorian lace. Palms
held up to the wet-nosed world.

Winter. Hatchet of cold off the marsh.

                                                    Alone

slumped at the kitchen table,
she closes her hand.

XIII

Untamed, the branches of a stone cherry
spiralling across a door. Like living hair, it winds and curls.

Bring us the smell of Norway maple. Scent
of orange leaves like dessert on our tongues.

The outside world's floating in wood-edged
squares set inside the window pane –

a fractured country,
foreign shore.

What survives the force
of ruin's tide? Look at the door frame:

tough as teeth. Knock wood.
It could break your hand.

XIV

Listen. This language is winter's. A primal
speech of branches clanking in wind.

Past words, you drop against the pillow, senseless
as lead. Fall like a stone through sleep's black water.

At dawn, the world's a mass
of snow.

Everything's
holding its tongue.

The dark bucket of Saturday night. Bodies bowed
around the table. Faces dim. Potato eaters.

Through the evening, voices broil and reach, melding
like wax.

Song is a white
candle.

XV

Rose-gold light shuttering through
a lens of broken leaves and needles –

the picture of peace it makes
on the snow.

Where wiry branches claw and wheel from ground,
lilac will burst into mauve temples of trance and languor.

In the end, everything says its name.
Then stops, and stills.

For decades, in a half-ring of eroded bricks
behind the shed, neglected rhubarb's waxed and greened.

In a patch of velvet shade underneath the rowan tree,
that forgotten air becomes so cool and sweet,

you can almost
drink it.

When spring comes,
I'll show you where.

XVI

After the worst of it, after the days of the black nets
that entangled you, that wrapped
themselves around your will as you lay

in the starched anonymity
of the new bed in the nursing home,

I see you at the end of the hall,
just reaching it – the white vinyl-
plastic window that gazed directly into the woods,

filling with wild green light.

You were bent and curved like a fish's
mouth, down-turned, ferning into
yourself as you gripped the sides of the hated walker,

hanging like an empty shirt.

I know you won't succeed in this, but there's
something in the measured gait,
the shuck forward, as if you could

escape the swelling sky of circumstance
if you just kept walking.

Like a man who's overdosed
and mustn't sleep, you swim your
ruined body forward, each glittering

step a sand-shoal
holding back the sea.

XVII

The white raw's
seeping in. The light –

the living room's drowned,
floating in shadows.

At the edge of the curtain,
day is an arsonist. A finger firing gold brocade.

They tell me my grandmother used to sit in the dressmaker's
shop, swaying in the cage of a wooden chair.

Behold: she talks to the world
with her eyes closed.

I hear voices. Dark tongues
moulting in air.

XVIII

In the kitchen, my stepmother's
boiling water for dishes.

Grey rain drumming. Maybe
there's time.

If I knew how, I'd unribbon it, unwind
myself from this dry cocoon.

From a snow-lined flowerbed
out front, a daffodil unfurls:

blank
as a toy sheriff's badge;

spring's empty glare's
too bright, sincere.

In the drafty house, alone with the heat
of a fiery glass on the kitchen table,

my grandmother wanted

the woollen coat
she could recognize.

XIX

To her, you were the bay-raised, bright-
eyed field. Dishevelled son.

Horses,
horses.

I'm telling you, family's
an old night, its chaos Miltonic.

The strong eastern winds will
come. The high tides.

On the rotting banks of the rising creek,
an ungodly brown collapsing; thrash –

there is no mercy
in the melt. Things flow.

At the water's edge, hard as cast-iron, a snarl
of tree roots darkly clinging.

It's no use; we're
under a white, vowelless sky;

the stars the stars
can't blazon through.

XX

Mounted under dusty glass upon
the wall, a shadowed, long, suspended moment –

a horse and a train are
about to collide.

In the damp loam of abandoned
family plains, in the marsh fields in the time-stained dark,

industry
and sinew fight.

The bright, hawk-taloned
blue of my grandfather's gaze.

Storm-shades
inside the painting.

The colour of sorrow
decrees in the house tonight,

nobody
shall sleep.

Awake in the narrow,
wooden bed, I'm listening –

like a faucet-
drip

the mindless
way the minutes pool –

emptiness, tutor my eye;
teach me how to fire my heart

into the whipped sky above
the hay.

Tintamarre:

the racket. Goddammit,
the noise.

When I first open my eyes in the flowered room at the end
of the hall, morning light's a grey feather.

April's heavy,
iron press.

How long have you
been waiting?

Perched at the edge of the bed
in your hunting vest at the nursing home,

the brand-new way
your shoulders stoop.

It's wafting through the upstairs rooms
like beige chiffon:

a dove's moody
funereal call –

       in a dream, someone moans,
       someone moans

we don't think; and
the moment comes –

you'll
fly alone.

XXII

The fine grace
of a skeleton key in the door reminds me.

My heart's become
a wary eye;

we cannot ride
this bald, apocalyptic sky.

Sorrowing in the green boat
of a leather recliner, you gaze into the fake wood floor.

In the disembodied
corridor, fluorescent voices hurry like torches;

night
sprawls –

      in the feral yard, the hawthorn's sharp-
      nailed branches clawing

buds pulsing, new worms scaling
empty air. What's hope?

A ruddy braid of morning light keeps winding
itself through the bottom rungs of a splintered chair.

XXIII

The sound of rain's
built a feathered nest in the unlit kitchen.

The day's heavy.
Damp as lungs.

From a greasy wire hanger hooked on a shining ledge
of pine moulding in the hall,

a cotton work-shirt
listlessly turns.

Don't stay in the safe,
uterine dark of the woodshed

like a ruined leaf
clinging to a pitchfork tine.

They say
there were horses here.

In the night, I've run
through the sun-washed fields of their manes in my dreams.

Tremble, and
be still –

there's a dirt-knowing
lining the silence.

It's all
the same.

XXIV

I'm still seeing you there.

Stationed at the kitchen table
in the frayed caul of a flannel jacket. Staring
avidly into the street through the front porch window,

as you gripped the sides
of the rooted table to ride a knife-

edged tide of pain.

On the green tile floor, an ocean
of tax statements and unpaid bills where
you shuffled your feet,

rustling back and forth as if they were leaves

and you were a child again
out on the marsh, pretending to scare
up ducks with your little dog. Clouds

coming apart like cotton; insects stoned
in the vacant heads of dandelions,
bedrooms of docile yellow.

You sat and drank, thinking of it, seeing it all,
religiously lifting the glass
of burnished gold to your mouth

and then setting it down as if
you were punctuating something.

The rhythm, the solemn flow
of the lifting and the pouring and the holding
of that liquid fire inside your mouth

like a moment of clear knowing: life
and death –

the rhythm of it, the flow of your own
breath like the wind through the folds of the blinds
in your childhood room when you finally

emptied it out and she was there.

You could feel the contours
of her face, the taut pull on the fine
skin of her cheekbones like basketball leather;

not like it is in the photograph
that's hanging in the den –

she's gazing out from the centre
of the shot: captain of the ladies' team,
her stark, adolescent face veiled by something that feels
    like smoke,

like boding, something was taking her even then
as she sits with the weathered
field ball between her hands like she's holding
the circumference of the known world

and stares through the empty
space of the glass partition that divides
the rooms, stares at you

lifting and lowering the glass
of liquid oblivion like she showed you to
when you learned

to drink, to swallow it all.

XXV

In the morning, the sheer lime-gold
of the honey locust.

Can your dulled heart
carry the weight of its spell?

Somewhere
on the High Marsh Road,

bits of sweet, unsellable hay felt like hourglass grit
in the funnel of my great-grandfather's hand.

I remember you sitting alone
in the dark. Wrapped in the gauze of twilight

the earthy brown neck of the bottle
a well into which you'd mysteriously dive.

Sound of crows. A sharp
serrated knife;

everything's ready
to brawl.

XXVI

Collapsed around the drain in the bathroom sink, a
tiny white violet's an exhausted dancer.

At dawn, the sudden grace of a ring-necked
pheasant wandering the garden rows;

he's a ruined king
looking for gold.

In the marrow, echoes of generations
falling: there could be more –

the dark thirst in the blood
is a clot that's still travelling the length of our lives.

Leave it be; the ants
will come again, invade.

I'm taking it back. I'm taking
the history we've twisted like sheets into rags.

That's the one white bone
I'll fight you for.

XXVII

On the wall, your hand faithfully walked the stations
of calendar pages. In emotive script, you hymned what came:

May snow, dry rot,
green shoots, rain.

Don't press the newborn tips
of these blue spruce needles: they'll shatter in a liquid sigh.

The solid noun of a toppled
box elder leafless on the thawing ground;

its body's a white bear,
a monarch downed.

Jagged sheen
of still-becoming leaves;

your eyes could sever
themselves on that green.

XXVIII

In a hurry, I sweep my hand across a light switch: nothing
happens. Haul the beige curtain. Rod falls to the floor.

On the branches of the ruddy pine, soft gelatinous
fingers of budding cones emerge like purple smoke

a genie pluming
forth.

I found my grandmother's jewellery box. It was
in the basement.

Elastic bands so old they've frayed still latch it together
as if rubber binding could hold in those secrets, that shame.

Give me the plainsong
of this unvarnished sill;

how it bears
the weight of light like water.

XXIX

On a darkened wall, diaphanous reflections from a tiny
chandelier: mauve-violet. Emerald. Gold;

lost moons that have
strayed from orbit.

Wild bells of tasselled lily-
of-the-valley.

This photograph doesn't give me
her voice.

On a moon blued stair,
she staggered –

grabbed for the waiting rail,
scuffled with empty air.

In the chilly, unfuelled night,
the abandoned garden shivers and burns.

XXX

I can see you at dusk, trawling the yard
with an ancient wheelbarrow, attuned to it all.

A scholar
of light and air.

In the silence of the living room, a squall
of sealed envelopes lies thickly on the couch like snow.

The kitchen was always your domain.
In the morning, the sink was filled with fins and tails,

smell of salmon flesh
and blood.

You're dying.

The last of the chokecherry
blossoms are gone;

there's nothing
on the lilac now.

XXXI

In the sink, the metal tap drips
once. Then, stops.

4 p.m. My stepmother's upstairs
asleep. When the sun begins to fall, she'll rise.

As I step from wildered garden rows,
I pause; shake out a shoe –

rose-cream petals
rain through air.

It's midnight. She's up. Sorting
through boxes for something to sell.

The moon's up, too,
greying the sill.

XXXII

Dark, mothering green
of heart-shaped lilac leaves.

Nothing's going
to hurt you now.

I can feel it in the cold backs
of the kitchen chairs: time's moved from here like pollen.

Flushed as a bride, you came in from the yard
clutching a basket of raspberries like a secret stash;

Promethean
cull.

Sullen grey of the lamp fixture
hanging at the top of the stairs –

circumstance
is a raging storm.

Light, light, light, light, light –

be the river
that runs through it now.

XXXIII

My stepmother's huddled on the couch
in the cold den with a broken heater turned to her waist.
Beneath a furry blanket, she floats in a reedy half-conscious
    sleep –

she is drowning. The day is like sand in her mouth.

In the dimness of the blind-drawn light,
with her grey-black hair cascading across the pillow,
she is a sea creature washed ashore,

a beached mermaid, a rebel daughter
who lies subterranean under the mass
of threadbare cotton blankets that she's heaped

upon herself like the shame
she has taken into her cells like oxygen.

Now, all she can breathe is water –
the clear gold of the cheap rye the taxi-driver's
brought to the door.

Where is her husband, you ask,
as anyone in their right mind would. Where is my father?

Washed into the trees he is at last, breathed
out like stale breath into the tall pines at the back
of the garden that stand and holler
and call out death though no-one hears.

I hear
and the hearing's like a curse.

I hear; it fills my head with water.

II

Say, sea,
Take me!
Emily Dickinson

NIGHTSHADE CLIMBING LIMBS
OF WHITE BIRCH

I

I waited for you in the dark
by the woodshed;

the moon's tongue
a blue flare in the pines.

On the beach road, a wound in the side of a fallen
spruce is a shelf for debris;

emptiness filling with field-
weeds and sand.

In the ditches, wild roses. The butterfly's
mouth. How long can the summer between us endure?

If you come, we'll sit at the table.
Stars can wait by the window;

we'll talk
the sky down.

You say you waited with me
inside you all winter.

The vacant
glass the night can be.

We're sweetly fed. Fat from each other's
letters scenting our hands.

In the morning, I can walk only steps before
being accosted: the sea's beauty –

once, the pockets
of my eyes were empty;

now,
they fill.

III

In the cabin, your voice on the phone
entwines me. Nightshade climbing limbs of white birch.

Evening's half-filled
cup on the table;

your knock at the door
a finished song.

Let's run through the marsh; let's
lay the length of our true selves down.

This big, sun-blanketed field is a bed
where the fragrant breath in our bodies will go.

When you leave, I want the ocean –
its jewels and its promise before the clock's metal returns.

A sudden black-
emerald glint:

bone-wheel of a ravaged
crow flickering on a seaweed mound.

We know it. Love is
a pirate's flag;

a wind-
torn wing.

Every ransomed moment's a prism
caught and held inside a palm.

Learn to weather hard rain – what's
untarnished gets whelmed,

buried. Revealed
again.

V

On the beach, the memory of your body's scent is a boat
riding the white salt waves.

At dawn, the ocean's
grey exhale. The first words.

Say what's
been.

This swale of minutes –
a fan falling open. Pleats biting, closing on air.

Night. October is filling the hour
with cold: a blanket of naught. Burying ground.

I'm still here. The beach town is deserted.
All the green and coinage gone.

In the morning, light rouses reed-heads in the marsh:
a glittering drawer of polished tines.

On the beach road, a gift –
the slender book a bark-slab makes;

the artistry
of empty sheets.

Dare to peel things back. There's magenta
on the underside. Real blood.

VII

You say you'll come, then don't. I tell you
I'll be here, then leave. Stars

reeling in their fiery dance. Above us,
all the music's found.

Damn this season, this catwalk
across a chasm,

the narrowing
of the coming days.

Take my hand and spin me
back to a time of grassy jade.

Tonight, the bare, big field's
a bowl. Echoes –

echoes – I'm tasting
your voice.

VIII

Be careful. This is a trance-state,
a fugue. Ophelia's death-stroll through wildflowers.

All day, I walked through the steady rain.
All day, I walked through the sky of your absence.

Late at night, in the wooden rafters, the hard wind rolls
like a child's body surfing known hills.

In cider-coloured water, collapsing
rushes buckle and swoon.

What is it we'll
give to each other? Words.

Trust the field's
better speaking.

IX

Listen: in the dark, the hollow clack
of cattail stalks against each other –

beige pages
erasing themselves.

You're gone.
The hours stretch like wasted dancers.

Moon, sun. Bodies
pirouette alone.

Drown all the words in the ocean;
the only true poem is the current's race and return.

The day's unwound. I force
myself to walk the starless road;

my skin's
disappearing in air.

X

In dawn-lit woods, go deeper.
Trunks clamour.

Splintered, splayed
in different ways.

Quiet, pewter silk of lichen. Muscled
backs of mushroom shelves.

This swatch of sober suede-brown
gale in the dying marsh reminds me I've paid.

Suddenly, everything's
calling. Roping my eyes –

the world's
adorned in ribbons.

XI

Stampeding through the weeds, the scarlet
noise of wild rose.

You're there. A bottle, an iron look,
and a canvas bag stuffed with rigging –

if I hand you a map,
can you find us a door?

Let's go to the green sea. Quick-
breathed and restless.

It could draw us out. It could
take us to shore.

XII

These threads
of old fire between us,

tenuous as the molten lace
the season's made of alder leaves.

Water, blood, skin,
forgiveness. The moon is a level eye in air.

On the dirt road, wind's high inside
the mighty pines. History

unribbons – inside that wail,
a braid unwinds.

In the ditches, clover
frozen to its stem;

memories
of lively mauve.

Take this white stone
with you.

I'll carry the weight of your kiss
in my bones.

III

We must unlearn the constellations to see the stars.
Jack Gilbert

RAVAGED

I

Jewelled by the dying light, the ruby-bodied gull's flying
determined into the sea.

Everything we've done is mustering on the horizon line,

a yellow eye staring and burning.

I want to be this vine of nightshade climbing like voices
into the trees.

The space between stars, the distance –

what's extraneous will be cindered away.

Time's fire is in our ears –

the ocean sighs, winding and curling.

II

The water's burnished heart-torn blue in the minutes
    before the light is gone.

I'm staying here to watch the ribbon-candy of the body
    spilling from this moon-snail shell.

O earth·

we're lost in a season of understanding;

the news is being received and absorbed.

To disappear, to *merge* –

once, there was a prescription for that.

Just stare at the world with all your being;

make of your body an eyeball and burn.

III

They follow the sea's movement. The broken-hearted,

the bereaved.

See that man with the ravaged face?

He stands at the edge of the waterline each day and stares,

his body terse as a question mark.

Go into the fields.

In the blur and churn of the coming days,

go ask the waning cattail stalks.

Resist soft beds of hibernation.

IV

In the morning, autumn's husky light floods protected salt
    marsh reeds;

for a minute, everything is gold.

On a dirt path through woods scheduled to be destroyed
    to build a massive RV park,

the bristle-brush of wild roses is standing straight up,
    stating its name.

In a clearing, broken bodies of sedges steep in brackish
    rust-orange water;

the air above the clotted pool sings like whiskey,

sharp as sex.

What is it to die?

V

The stricken wind. The gale-savaged trees –

greed has stripped us, rendered us bare.

This oyster shell's so dry, it clatters in your hands;

the intricacies of its mauve-edged cities.

Ripped flag of a crow-wing stuck in a rotting mound of sand.

Detritus of fast-food wrappers and bone –

everything's curling in on itself.

The diagnosis –

the weight.

The tensed

legs and

the clenched hands.

The pillow's

snow beneath their cheek.

VII

I met the man with the grief-torn face.

He was standing on the rotting boardwalk staring into the
cattail fields.

We don't see the birds anymore; we used to see them;

they had a patch of bright orange on their shoulders.

We used to call them warrior birds.

In slow, careful stages, the ocean greys.

Something settles in me.

VIII

In a beige shadow on the torso of a dune, I lay without
   thinking for maybe an hour,

arcs of beach-grass cathedraled above me.

It will all unwind like ribbon—

down to the core of the selfish will around which we have
   threaded and woven the world.

The weather's changed – we're cast

into this storm. Rain and fire coming down from the ceiling.

IX

We're wed to the swing and the sway of the ocean,

its swell and its tides heading straight for the shore.

In the purple gloaming, I can only see your outline in the
distance,

beloved as a known country.

The night is without stars. The future's

a map with the names of the cities erased.

In the dying light,

there is only the soft, animal form of our bodies,

turning to walk towards each other,

and the ageless pounding of the water –

the rhythm of its burgeoning speech.

NOTES AND ACKNOWLEDGMENTS

I am grateful to the Access Copyright Foundation, Arts Nova Scotia, and the Writers' Trust of Canada for the financial support that enabled me to write these poems. I am also grateful to Arts Nova Scotia for the Public Art Funders Creative Residency grant that allowed me to live and work in New Brunswick for three months during the initial stages of this project. My sincere thanks to Gretchen Fitzgerald and Heidi Verheul of Sierra Club Canada (Atlantic Chapter) for their enthusiastic support of this project and for their assistance with fieldwork.

Tintamarre (meaning "din" or "racket") is what French Acadian settlers called the Tantramar Marshes because of the sounds of migratory birds that frequented there.

"Nightshade Climbing Limbs of White Birch" was a finalist in the Gwendolyn MacEwen Poetry Competition. Sections from this sequence were also published in the special *Biophilia* edition of *The Dalhousie Review* (Winter 2020) and in *The Fiddlehead*, 75th anniversary edition (Spring 2020).

Sections from "Rags of Night in Our Mouths" appeared in *Wild Green Light* (Pottersfield Press, 2021), a collaborative book of poems with David Adams Richards. Section XVI of "Rags of Night in Our Mouths" appeared in *The Fiddlehead* as "The Walk." It was also featured in the Academy of American Poets/League of Canadian Poets "Poem in Your Pocket Day" booklet, and it appeared as a postcard, as a recording, and in the online dispatch *Poetry Pause*. My thanks to the editors and staff involved in each of these publications.

Warmest thanks to Allan Hepburn for his editorial suggestions and also for his kindness and support. My thanks, as well, to Jacqueline Davis, Kathleen Fraser, Jennifer Roberts, Carolyn Smart, and everyone at McGill-Queen's for their enthusiasm and help.

For their generosity, encouragement, and support over the years, I am deeply grateful to Mark Abley, Sandra Barry, Brian Bartlett, Allan Cooper, Sarah Emsley, Basma Kavanagh, Genevieve Lehr, Alexander MacLeod, David Adams Richards, Peter Sanger, Robyn Sarah, Vanessa Shields, and Jan Zwicky. Special thanks to Janet Baker, Kimberly Berry, Catherine Hamilton, Catherine, Ashton, and John Hennigar-Shuh, Joanne Jardine, Jill MacLean, Cynthia Maillet, Scott Nickerson, Dianne and John Oldham, Janice Plimmer, Reg Richard, Roxanne Smith, Sandi Wheaton, and Joanne Wise for lighting the way.

Special love for my special family: to Paul Émile d'Entremont and to Jay Wheaton, beautiful son. Profound love and gratitude to Robert Christian. For making everything possible.

*

"Rags of Night in Our Mouths" is for my father. The spring-based ghazals XVII–XXIII are dedicated to Paul Émile d'Entremont with thanks for saving them. "Nightshade Climbing Limbs of White Birch" and "Ravaged" are for the Northumberland Strait shoreline that runs along the plage de l'Aboiteau (Aboiteau Beach) in Cap-Pelé, New Brunswick.

*

This book is for my family, and for the ghosts.